# TOWARDS A DYNAMIC SOCIAL DEVELOPMENT

# TOWARDS A DYNAMIC SOCIAL DEVELOPMENT

J. Okechuku Nzelibe

**VANTAGE PRESS**
New York / Los Angeles

FIRST EDITION



Published by Vantage Press, Inc.
516 West 34th Street, New York, New York 10001

Manufactured in the United States of America
ISBN: 0-533-08227-7

Library of Congress Catalog Card No.: 88-90334

To Oberlin Friends

# Contents

**Part IV. Religious Development**

# Acknowledgements

Thanks to Oberlin College, where I began my educational career in the United States.

The orientation exercise in Oberlin would tell any foreign student what Oberlin stands for: Oberlin's activities in rescuing a black American who was about to be lynched in a neighboring city; Oberlin's position as the first liberal arts college to admit women and blacks; and Oberlin students' activities in voter-registration campaigns in the Southern United States of America. All these activities spell out *American liberalism.* My gratitude goes to Oberlin friends who were my guardians in the United States and who helped pay my way. Especially I would mention friends like the Reverend Dr. and Mrs. D. L. Anderson of the physics department, Oberlin College; Bishop T. Jones, then rector of the Episcopal church in Oberlin; and the members of Christ Episcopal Church in Oberlin. Mr. and Mrs. D. Polhemus, the former Director of Alumni Oberlin College, and the late Doris Morton, my house mother, should also be mentioned.

I am thankful to the professors in the economics department—B. Lewis, W. Hellmuth, and T. Dernburg—and also the late Professor N. Anagnos of Howard University's department of economics. Through their lectures, all the professors made me absorb the real practical side of economic principles applicable to developing countries.

I appreciate the contributions of Professor Yinger of the sociology department and the late Professor Long of the department of religion. All these courses expanded my knowledge in social science.

My gratitude goes to those who have helped me in many ways: Mr. and Mrs. T. K. Filipiak, my father- and mother-in-law; Mr. L. McHugh and Mr. Dave Ziegler, my college roommates; and Dr. and Mrs. Larry Keefer.

I am also grateful to the Professor E. C. O. Ilogu, who, although a cousin, has continued to advise me in any period of time and through whom my traveling to the United States was made possible.

Finally, I very much appreciate my family for their contributions. My wife's faithfulness gave me support in time of difficulty, and she questioned some of my ideas when they were not clear. My two older children—a daughter and a son—with their innocent approach to the world gave me criticisms the younger generation would give. My two youngest children, with their childlike activities and questions, made some impact on my knowledge.

Thanks to the class of 1963 for their friendly fellowship.

I am grateful to Mrs. E. Omeke, for her devoted work in typing the manuscript.

To all the friends and relatives not mentioned, I owe many thanks.

# Preface

*Towards a Dynamic Social Development* is aimed at the development of undeveloped countries. Nigeria is the area of this research. That is why most examples are taken from there. The book will be useful for students of economic development. The book stresses that imitation cannot develop a nation. The inference is drawn from the development of developed nations.

This book will also help the governments of developing countries know the stages of development and the priority areas in development. Development will be practical and not theoretical. We know what is going on and we see the result of what is going on.

# TOWARDS A DYNAMIC SOCIAL DEVELOPMENT

# Part I

# Historical Section

# Chapter 1
# Introduction

Man's remarkable records of his never-ending search for a means to explain the world about him through the use of reason began with the Greeks. The reason often begins with questions, and efforts to find the answers to the questions result in reasoning. I often ask why it is that efforts to develop the Third World countries and Africa in particular for all these years have not been successful. There are enormous resources in these countries. The cosmic system is in operation in these countries, as in developed countries. There are learned people, both aliens and citizens. But all efforts to develop them remain futile.

Early Western colonial development revealed that all social developments go together. The British in Africa came with trade, colonial administration, and religion; where one aspect was weak, others would make up for it. Economic development alone will not be successful. It must go with other developments.

The Western countries' development was a break from the old socioeconomic structure. The socioeconomic disturbances had their roots in the beliefs of the people, the production and distribution of the resources, and the relationship between the people and their lords—that is, religious, economic, and political disturbances.

*Development* is used very loosely. There are mixtures of other concepts in the usage of *development*. People mix imitation and building on an already laid foundation with *de-*

*velopment.* In order to have the real philosophy and concept of *development,* there is a need to think of nonexistence of the developed phenomenon, or to think of the indigenous cultures on which the development will begin, or to think of the similar cultures that exist somewhere else on which the development will take root. All these thoughts will be developed to have a separate and novel cultural pattern which will give them the name of the producer. They will be the product of the producer and not an imitation of another producer.

In this book attention will be on religious, economic, and political developments. These are the phenomena that will help to realize the kind of social development the writer is stressing. To define *development* I will first define *knowledge.* Knowledge is the digested information produced by a person. The digestion will be inside the person. The information comes from the books we read, the discussions we have with people, what we see, and what we hear. All these are digested inside us, and what we produce out of the digested materials is knowledge. Not only educated people have knowledge. Inventors and entrepreneurs have knowledge, that is why they bring new things into existence.

Development is the ability to apply the knowledge and assemble the available indigenous resources to produce a finished product. The knowledge employed will be that of the nationals, and the resources are from the nation. No nation develops another nation. But nationalized people can develop their nationalized countries. For example the United States of America, Canada, Australia, South Africa, and so on, were developed by other nationals who migrated into those countries and become nationalized members of the countries.

Dynamic social development will include the most important areas of social development, and it will try to include dynamic social checks and balances which will help to provide a stable, steady development. Development will be practiced in stages of priorities according to the country's cultural background and resources.

# Chapter 2
# Western Historical Development

The history of Western development philosophically, economically, and politically will give an insight to the development of other countries. The developing countries will thus be exposed to many things in front of them. They will know what to avoid and what to accept in their trend of development. The schools of thought will be taken in their order of existence.

## Physiocrats

Physiocrats were the French group of philosophers in about the eighteenth century who propounded a theory that land is the source of all wealth. From this they maintained that the only productive sector of the society was the farmers who worked on the land. This brought concentration on agriculture and land.

## Feudalism

The feudal lords were the owners of the land. The land which was the source of all wealth became the property of the feudal lords. The lords became the owners of the wealth of the society. They allocated the resources of the society to any person they wanted. In addition to the feudal lords' land control, there was centralized religion. The religious heads had control of the people while the feudal lords had control of the land. When these two groups had agreement of ideas, the whole society would be controlled by them. This was the condition of Europe in the middle ages. There was economic backwardness due to the centralized religion and centralized ownership of the land of feudal lords.

## Mercantilism

The growth of trade due to the mobility of the peasants created another group of people known as mercantilists. The contact with the outside world made the mercantilists question the position of the feudal lords and the religious leaders. Religious reformation and mercantilism with their novelties changed the attitude of Europe and created nationalist spirit and faith in government intervention in the economy. This group of people was not from the owners of the land or the gentry, but from the lower class of people, who found virtues in thrift and industry. These became the bourgeoisie, who were very important in the history of economic development of Europe. They were the entrepreneurs and risk takers of Europe. They did much to achieve national economic unity. Mercantilism was responsible for saving and investment. That spearheaded the excess of production of domestic demand. The surplus over the domestic demand became the exports which developed into foreign markets.

## Classical School

The classical school attacked the mercantalists because of their faith in government intervention in the economy. The classical school had the policy of laissez-faire. The school never believed in interventions in economic matters. The division of labour, production, and export would be a nation's comparative advantage. Free trade would be granted to all and a free market for all commodities would be practiced. All these would be controlled by price. These led to laws of supply and demand and price theory. The classical school believed that self-interest of the bourgeoisie and entrepreneurs would control the economic activities better than the intervention of the government. The entrepreneurs and bourgeoisie became the capitalists who provided the savings and capital. By the theory of wage, and the theory of supply and demand, the availabilty of capital and the numbers of the labour force in market became the determinants of wages. More labour forces in the job market would reduce the wages of labour, and less labour in the job market would increase the labour wage.

## Keynes

The Keynesian revolution cannot be easily applied in the developing countries. It is a revolution of full employment economy. Keynes attacked the classical school for the laissez-faire theory as a panacea which can solve economic problems. Keynes maintained that the things hindering full employment are the problems of money, unemployment, and depression. He said that inadequate demand is due to insufficient purchasing power. In order to solve the problems of depression, underemployment and unemployment will be solved. By underemployment he means that the employed labour force does not have an adequate wage to satisfy its purchasing power. By unemployment he means that there are many economic wastes. For example, those who are eligible to be employed are not employed and for that their productive powers with other resources are not exploited. Keynes did not believe that there could be a real inflation without full employment. He maintained that increase in wages would increase spending and the increase in spending would increase production. Or increase in wages would increase saving and increase in saving would increase investment. So any increase in wages would cause an accumulative effect on growth. So a decrease in wages would result in depression.

## Socialism

Socialism attacked capitalism. Socialism pointed out the exploitation of man by man. The capitalists exploited the labour force and because of that, inequality in the distribution of productivities was created. So it tried to emancipate the proletariat from the bondage of the capitalists. Fredrick Engels said, "Both Christianity and the worker's socialism preach forthcoming salvation from the bondage and misery; Christianity places this salvation in a life beyond, after death, in heaven; socialism places it in this world in a transformation of society."[1] Socialism is a stage of development. Like the Keynesian revolution it is difficult to apply it in developing nations because it is not a beginning stage of development. Marx and Engels in their book *Basic Writings on Politics and Philosophy* said, "The first direct attempts of the proletariat to attain its own ends, made in times of universal excitement when feudal society was being overthrown, these attempts necessarily failed, owing to the then undeveloped state of the proletariat, as well as to the absence of the economic conditions for its emancipation, conditions that had yet to be produced, and could be produced by the impending bourgeois epoch alone."[2]

1. Marx and Engels, *Basic Writing on Politics and Philosophy*, ed. Lewis S. Feur (n.p.: Aucho Books, 1959), 168.

2. *Ibid*, 37.

# Chapter 3
# Historical Development Philosophy

From the early Western and Eastern philosophers it will be seen that the developing countries of today have a lot to do. They have not built a school of thought, and they have not studied realistically the true path of development of developed nations. What the developing countries do is to imitate the already developed cultures of developed nations. But this is very difficult to do. The developing countries will first develop their philosophies based on their cultures. These indigenous philosophies will build schools of thought that will give a shape to the country's development. Development has its philosophy. Society can never begin development. The beginning of development is from an individual. When individuals formulate a development scheme, test it, and perfect it, then the society will be developed.

From the study of the history of economic development of the developed nations one finds some facts about development. When a country will have the same level of earning. Farming is the industry. Everyone does it. No one depends on another person for existence. The leaders are religious heads and elderly people. They are few and cannot form a group or a class. The society becomes a classless society.

The development begins when someone can find a different way of life, a different means of production. The whole society cannot do that, it is a very few people that will be involved in development activities. In some cases the beginners of developmental activities are neglected, and some are called names and mocked. Since development is the function of individuals and not society, socialism is not the philosophy of development. Socialism cannot be attributed to the underdeveloped society because of its classless structure. Socialism has a very high moral integrity which a beginner can never acquire. It is very difficult for one to perform for the good of society. People are selfish by nature; not until they reach a kind of social maturity can they perform for the good of the society. The subsistence level society cannot be looked upon as an area of socialism. People who have not been subjected to the riches of the world will never think of socialism as a philosophy until they are exposed to the riches and their temptations. In developing countries many of them like to be affiliated to socialism, but when the riches multiply, there is tendency towards accumulation, so that they will be called capitalists.

Capitalism is the philosophy that encourages development. Since an individual has rights over what he possesses, and he is entitled to what he can invent or innovate, the inventive mind is prevalent over the individuals and not society. By pursuing the self-interest of the individuals, the society is built.

The history of economic development in developed countries reveals that land is the first capital, and that philosophy and religion developed around the land. The physiocrats regarded land above all other things, and so farmers were highly respected. Feudalism regarded land very highly, but the land became apportioned to a few individuals. These became lords. Mercantalism challenged the feudal lords by building economic power and created faith in government. The mercantalists were the progenitors of the modern economy. They developed wealth through trade, and they created faith in the government, thus developing a national feeling.

The classical school created faith in the people and destroyed the faith in the government's intervention in economy. What they did was to create capitalism. Economic power went back to the people. This time it was not like the feudal lords who possessed power through the land. The capitalists possessed capital power through the means of production.

At any event of change, the old school of thought or philosophy looks upon the new philosophy as an enemy because it endangers its existence.

The bourgeoisie that destroyed the relationship tying man to his master left man alone without the moral attachment to his master. Such freedom without means of sustenance could lead to a worse kind of slavery than before. so the bourgeoisie tried to solve the condition it created by the destruction of the system of the society. It created jobs for the freed men, i.e. the proletariat. Marx defined the bourgeoisie as the class of modern capitalists, owners of the means of social production and employers of wage labour. He defined the proletariat as the class of modern wage labourers who have no means of production of their own, but who are reduced to selling their labour power in order to live.[3]

The history of social development in Europe exposed the fact that any revolution that could not solve the problem it created by revolution must receive a counterrevolution. Similarly any country that cannot solve the problems it created by throwing the colonial powers out of the country would be in danger of instability. The developing countries in order to be stable would study these problems in the history of developed nations, and would try to avoid the areas of development that would bring instability. This is what dynamic social development tries to do.

The developing countries try to imitate the visible sides of development as seen in the developed countries, but the

3. *Ibid*, 7.

invisible sides are neglected. The visible sides are the development of roads, building industries, and other enjoyable goods and services. But the invisible sides are the philosophies that will prepare the minds for the development of the visible sides. The reason is that these philosophies do not provide riches. History revealed that philosophers' contributions do not enrich them. When philosophers propound their philosophical beliefs, expressions, and reasonings, they raise questions that can make them be hated and even persecuted. But after their sufferings the society will enjoy the fruits of their labour. Socrates was ordered to take poison because he prejudiced the mind of the people with his thinking. Christ was crucified because of his philosophical views. He questioned the existence and performance of the old school of thought. Mohammad was neglected because of his views. Because philosophy does not bring wealth, the developing countries put much emphasis on the visible sides of development from whence wealth comes and ignore the invisible sides. Philosophy is very much needed to prepare the future generations for the trend of future events.

Mercantilism created a philosophy that destroyed the religious dependence of the middle ages and created nationalistic spirit and faith in the government. This does not mean that religion of the middle ages as we know it was destroyed. But it means that more facts were revealed in the knowledge of religion bringing it from what it was to what it should have been to help the development of Europe. The people of the middle ages were educated in this philosophy, and they freed themselves from the attachment to feudal lords and the gentry and freed their minds from the religious dogmas that bound them to poverty. Each school of thought liberated the society and redirected it to the area of its philosophy. Hence the physiocrats' land concept made the land the ultimate reality of production. The classical school's idea of laissez-faire took government's powers of intervention in economy and gave it to the people's power of self-interest. The arbitrator became the free market in which supply, demand, and price rules. Capitalism became the power and capitalists the rulers. The philosophy of socialism was that of salvation: salvation from the class that imprisoned the working class. The religion of socialism was the unity of the working class. The religion was the unity of the working class to free itself from the slavery of the dominating class. The dynamic social development will look into the errors of the past social developments and try to devise another pattern of development to bring more understanding between people. What developed into an uncontrollable accumulation of wealth stemmed from the possession of equipment and land. The farmers of old sold their labour to the feudal lords and the bourgeois who bought and enslaved them. The proletariat had no land and no equipment. The lords and the bourgeois possessed the land and equipment. At the distribution of the proceeds the bourgeoisie got the largest share because of the equipment. The proletariat being enslaved had no say. A farmer in the developing countries of today in order to be able to pull his weight in resource distribution will have the control of his equipment, his land, and his crops. This will allow most of the proceeds to go to the farmer. The designing of different sizes of equipment with different prices will help the individual farmer to possess the one that he can buy and the one he can maintain. The governments of the developing countries will try to undertake the manufacturing of industrial equipment. This will help to avoid the domination of the proceeds by very few individuals who would finance the equipment. The system of land tenure will be such that a professional farmer will have access to where to farm. The dynamic social development will include the development of values to avoid accumulation of proceeds by some individuals to such a degree as to create class antagonisms. Economic class system will be avoided because all resources of production are not in the condition of encouraging much accumulation. Wise fiscal policy will rationally redistribute the excess proceeds which would have accrued to the individuals illegally. Adequate checks and balances will bring stability to social acquisition so that an acceptable degree of satisfaction will be enjoyed by the people. Man will look at man as man and not as servant or tool of production. The worker will work with zeal to satisfy his conscience and not to cheat.

# Chapter 4
# African Socialism

Many intellectuals from all over the world: Europe, Russia, and the United States, have questioned the reality of African socialism. Many scholars have tried to show that the system of African culture and development cannot be associated with socialism. But many leaders of African countries are proving that the African system is socialistic. The views of African leaders' about African socialism originated from the fact that African society has no social classes and that the peasant community offers a subsistence level of living within the culture of extended relationships.

In dealing with African socialism, much stress will be placed upon the ideas of African leaders who profess socialism. For example Senghor, Nkrumah, and Nyerere will be dealt with. Before I go further an attempt will be made to define socialism. Socialism like all other philosophies is defined according to the ideas of the practitioners. But here an effort should be made to collect the isomorphisms that will help to give a general definition of socialism. In order to be able to make a logical definition, the four trends in African socialist theory as defined by A. Fenner Brockway[4] will be taken.

1. Communism or Marxism-Leninism
2. African Marxism
3. African pragmatic socialism
4. African democratic socialism

4. A. Fenner Brockway, *African Socialism* (London: The Bodley Head, 1963), 19.

The communists are active but have failed to acquire power in the African national movement or state. Marxist-Leninist ideology has risen mostly in ex-French colonies that were influenced by the French communist party. These are scattered in Algeria, Senegal, Guinea, Mali, the Cameroons, and in the Central African Republic. Marxist-Leninism insists on scientific socialism which is defined by class struggle, dictatorship of the proletariat, and dialectical materialism. All socialism which falls short of these values is regarded as utopian socialism by Marxist-Leninists. African Marxism could be found in Ghana, Guinea, and Mali whose leaders were strongly influenced by Marxism. They repudiated the class struggle, but shared with the communist countries in a monolithic state structure and authoritarian methods. In their views the Marxist-Leninist idealogy cannot fit in the cultural society of Africa, which is dominated by extended relationships, subsistence living and high religious participation. The African pragmatic socialists are dominant in the United Arab Republic, Tunisia, Senegal, Dahomey and Tanzania. They reject all the values of scientific socialism.

The African democratic socialists combine personal rights with economic collectivism as Jomo Kenyata summed it up in their manifesto: "Our achievement of independence, for which we have struggled so long will not be an end in itself. It will give us the opportunity to work unfettered for the creation of a Democractic African Socialist Kenya. *Democratic* because we believe that only in a free society can each individual develop his talents most fully to serve his fellow citizens. *African* because our nation must grow organically from what is indigenous, whilst adapting that which is suitable from other cultures from East and West. We must give our people pride and self-respect building upon all that is good and valid in our traditional society. *Socialist* because political freedom and equality are not enough; our people have the right to be free from economic exploitation and social inequality."[5]

From the above comments it will be seen that there is a great dichotomy in defining socialism in Africa. African leaders do not accept the Marxist socialism which dominated the Western view of socialism. Since African countries do not possess the qualities necessary for Marxist-Leninist socialism, they adopted a different kind of socialism. The Kenya African National Union (KANU) defines the function of their socialism in this say: "The government will itself initiate industries for the manufacture of finished articles from the agricultural produce of the country, but otherwise it will provide incentives to private investment since it will not have the available finance. It announces, however, that it will have no time for those who make large profits in Kenya and then fail to invest them in the country, and that it will exert a wide measure of control on the economy in the interest of the nation."[6]

Since African countries are poor, that is, they have limited resources, and since they want to develop the incentive attitude among their people, private enterprise is encouraged. This deviates from the theory of socialism in which all production is for the society. The common element in African socialism and Marxist-Leninist socialism is that all think about the society, but principles of how to care for the society differ.

## Summary

### Economically

Concerning the economy of Africa, I shall quote what Walter H. Drew said in his article, "How Socialist Are African Economies?" He said, "If the measure of socialism is the extent to which the state controls the production and disposition of

5. Kenya African National Union (the ruling political party in Kenya), 23.
6. *Ibid*, 24.

goods and services, Africa is probably less socialist than the United States. The U.S. government directly supplies and consumes about twenty percent of the U.S. national income, and by pervasive and complex regulatory devices over the remaining eighty percent of the economy, it strongly influences production and the disposal of production. Such a degree of government participation and direction is rare in Africa. This is not because African countries are committed by doctrine to less intervention in economic activity, but because their government administrative apparatuses are relatively weak. This is because popular resistance to detailed intimate central government direction of economic behaviour is still strong, and above all, because most African economic activity is still precapitalist based on the community organized life of the extended family or clan rather than on individual or corporate efforts to accumulate private wealth."[7] African economies are at present mixed economies of subsistence level or precapitalistic and money economies or capitalistic economies. The only nation in Africa that tried socialism but failed was Ghana. From its failure it is seen that Africa is not ripe for socialism because:

1. There is no accumulation.
2. There is no skilled man power.
3. There are not enough risk takers or entrepreneurs.
4. There are many avenues of innovation.

**Politically**

From many writers it is seen that Africans have started only recently to think of their countries as nations. The theory of fatherland and tribal feelings dominated African life. The

7. Walter H. Drew, "How Socialist Are African Economics?" *African Report*, Vol. 8 No. 5 (May 1963): 11. (Copyright 1963 by the African-American Institute. Reprinted by permission of *African Report*.)

governments do not care for their citizens. Extended families are responsible for the well-being of their relatives. Since nationalism is absent in Africa, there is no possibility for an individual to respect the nation and surrender his rights to the nation as is done in socialist countries. Since the state has little or no power, it cannot do away successfully with the institution of private ownership. So any attempt to nationalize what belongs to individual Africans will meet with popular resistance.

## Philosophically

The philosophies of African leaders agree with the philosophies of capitalist nations held when they were building their countries, that is, the self-interest of Adam Smith expressed in the *Wealth of Nations* and self-interest with responsibility of J. M. Clark in *Alternative to Serfdom*. These will be compared with Senghor's humanization and Nyerere's self-reliance. Also the philosophy of dialectics is manifested in two ways:

1. When it is attributed to class it gives interpretation to socialism, but
2. When it is attributed to an individual or thing it deviates from socialism. Therefore any philosophy that stresses individualism is antisocialism.

## Internationally

Within Africa, African socialistic countries are subversive to other African countries and militant in view. They want immediate decolonization from Westerners by force. They lose confidence in the African socialists. The Westerners withhold loans and aid, and investments also decrease. Since African countries have export economies, the reduction of African exports to Western countries results in an imbalance of trade and distortion in African economies. The Eastern bloc tends to export African products to areas where Africans export their products. The result is that Africans find themselves competing with their own products. The Chinese want a place to export their surplus labour. Africa has nothing in common with China, because there are opportunities in Africa and it is not overpopulated as is China.

Socialism has a very high standard of culture and a high morale which Africa does not yet possess. Ideally it represents a moral sacrifice which will make an individual give all his or her services to the state.

Since the African culture is not that of socialism, and since Africans want to be neutral, there is no reason why they should accept either Western or Eastern philosophies which are not identical to African philosophy. Vernor Mckay in *African Diplomacy* said, "While the cold war specialist tends to call nonalignment a function of bipolarity the Africanist regards it as a manifestation of Africanism."[8] By the Charter of the Organization of African Unity they agreed in article III, section 7, to a policy of nonalignment with regard to all blocs. There is no reason for accepting socialism in Africa since the policy of nonalignment is against it. In my opinion the best name for African culture and philosophy is Africanism as Mckay called it. This is a neutral name which best suits African cultures and philosophy.

8. Vernon McKay, *African Diplomacy*, 1966 (Praeger, Inc.), 16.

# Part II

# Economics

# Chapter 5
# Economic Development

Having a choice is one thing but making a choice is another. Having a choice of foreign goods is one thing but making a choice of home goods is another. Having a choice of foreign goods is good but making a choice of home goods is better. But above all having a choice in perfect home goods is the best because having is making.

## The Roots of Development

### Peace

Peace of mind makes a person stable—a person will be in a position of reasoning and thinking. Peace of mind makes a person's reasoning constructive and innovative. There will be a chain of reasoning and a chain of answering. The people become creative. These chains of reasonings and answerings are the beginning of development in a society. Individual peace results in a collective peace—the peace of a nation.

### Pax Romana

Pax Romana is the Roman peace. The peace that gave Rome and the world a long steady time of thinking and reasoning. This peace built Rome to be the mother of the world development and civilization, which gave her the world empire. Caesar became the ruler of the whole world. This peace built a network of roads in the Roman empire which made us say that "All roads lead to Rome." Through these roads the civilization flowed out. Religion of Christianity was spread throughout the world. Palestine—where Christ laboured, died, and rose from the dead—did not inherit the glory of His works because there was no peace in Palestine. The Church became the Roman Church. These are the elements and prices of peace. Dynamic social development will have its foundation on peace.

### Pax Britanica

Rome could not hold the peace. There were internal and external disturbances, so she lost the control of the peace and she lost the motherhood of the world to the British. The British peace reigned. The peace discussed here is national peace and not world peace. The British national peace gave an overflow of civilization to other parts of the world.

Peace that built the British empire gave an overflow of civilization to the British colonies. The worst disturbance to development is internal disturbance. The British empire became the mother of the world. The empire on which the sun never set. British peace helped her to rule successfully her colonies in Africa, Asia and other areas.

### Unity

Peace brings understanding. The mind becomes clear of evil thinking. A person will create in himself or in herself the conditions of approachability. Group actions become possible. A person becomes agreeable to his or her fellows. As

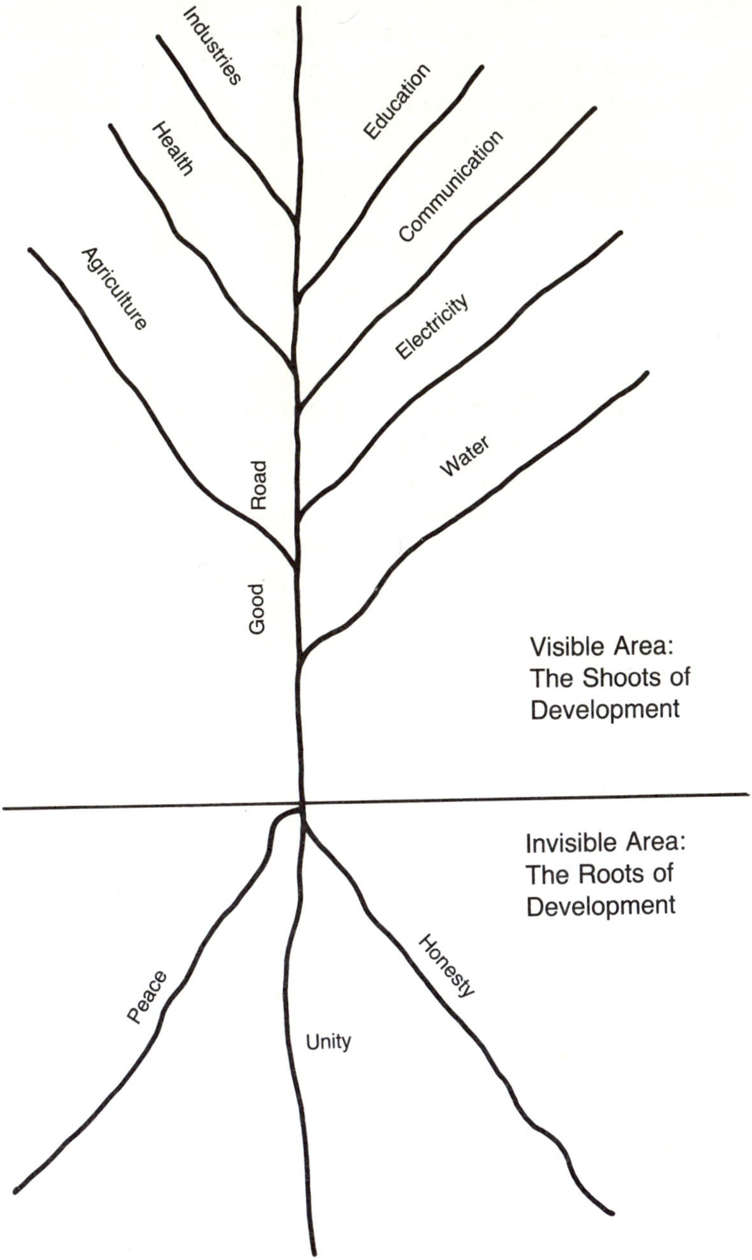


**Development Tree**

many as have created mutual understanding are bound together with rope of peace; this is the unity. These people that are bound together become a nation. This is why nationalism is the religion of a nation. The religion of unity is the religion of constructive action, in other words, the religion of development.

## Honesty

Peace begets unity and unity begets honesty. Peace works in the minds of individuals. It prepared the people for group action. It brings people together. People when so united will work with mutual understandings. Mutuality in understanding is honesty—the condition in which one trusts one's honest conscience. No one distrusts; there is no scepticism and no suspicion. These conditions help citizens to invest. They explore all areas and try to bring into existence that which is not there. This is the development of the area.

## Agriculture

Agriculture is the beginning stage of production development. No nation can really develop her economy in the absence of agricultural products. The British government went all over the world in search of raw materials. Today it is not really very possible to import all the raw materials needed in order to develop. So any nation that wants development will first develop her agriculture. Developed agriculture will have surplus products. Economic development will begin with the surplus products provided for by developed agriculture. Economic development will explore what to do with the surplus products.

Land is the area of agricultural practices. Soil will receive the first attention in development. Healthy rich soil is that which can give productive crops. The richness of the soil depends on the bacteria and other chemicals in the soil. Soil engineers will study and analyze the soil. The knowledge of the soil condition will help in the knowledge of the types of crops to grow there. Advantaged areas in crops will specialize in those crops. Development encourages specialization.

Indiscriminate burning of farm lands reduces the quality of the soil. Agricultural development will deal with the methods of preserving the richness of the soil and of specializing in the crops according to the soil analysis. The existing indigenous crops will first be developed. Agricultural development will include these areas:

1. Improving method of cultivation.
2. Improving the equipments of cultivation.
3. Choice of seeds.
4. Choice of livestocks.

## Improving Method of Cultivation

Developing nations practice mixed farming, that is, planting at a place different crops some of which may not grow together. The developed agriculture will introduce soil-advantaged crops to their areas and also plant together crops that can grow well together. The developed cultivation will also practice planting many seasonal crops more than once in a year through use of irrigation. Development will also include adding some chemicals and organic materials to enrich the soil. These will encourage planting yearly in a piece of land. This is very good for the area where land is scarce and where vegetable cultivation is practiced.

## Equipment Improvement

The dynamic social development maintains that a farmer must have land to farm, and he must be in control of his equipment and possess crops to be planted. All these are the measures to avoid dehumanization of farmers. A farmer who possesses all the equipments and materials to farm must be in control of his proceeds. The equipment will be well designed to suit the kind of soil. It will be such that a farmer will be able to buy and to manipulate it. In Nigeria, a designed equipment like a lawn mower will help the Nigerian farmers. Equipment loaning is not very advisable. Experience shows that a borrower of equipment may not be able to secure one before the planting season expires. So a farmer must possess his tools of farming, his land, and his crops.

## Choice of Seeds

Developed farming will develop the indigenous crops first. The development includes healthy seeds, large seeds, and those that taste good. That is development in life, size, and taste. There will be also introduction of healthy seeds from other areas which will be suitable to the soil where they are introduced.

## Choice of Live Stock

The climate of Nigeria favours live stock production. The live stock are left to feed themselves; there is no adequate care for them. There is no cattle feed in Nigeria. Cattle farmers walk from place to place in search of food for the cattle. The cattle-rearing industry will be developed when the food for the cattle is developed. The planting of fodder, hay, and other grasses will be introduced. In addition to that, the indigenous grasses can be cured and prepared for the cattle. The development of cattle feed will encourage a careful attention to the cattle. The cattle rearers do not treat the cattle well. The cattle are flogged. Such treatments will deter the development of the cattle. With a very kind treatment and good feeding, milking cattle can be developed in Nigeria. The fact that Nigeria cannot produce enough milk is due to the nature of the cattle and treatment given to the cattle. When the cattle are well treated, that is, when they are made to stay at a place and be fed, there will be a good production of milk and tender beef. The cattle farm industry like poultry industry will be improved in production. Poultry farmers now get regular production of eggs, unlike the old periodical egg production. The improvement is due to care and feeding of the poultry. Care and proper feeding of cattle will increase the milk production. This will bring development in allied milk industries such as cheese.

**Poultry Industry**

The poultry industry will take off as soon as there is a steady supply of good quality feed. The poultry industry is the livestock industry that has started very well. But it was disturbed due to lack of steady supply of good quality feed. Agricultural development is the revolution in the raising of indigenous food so as to create surplus. Developed agriculture can feed the people and the industries and still get surplus for export. If this is not so, the agriculture is *not* really developed. The agricultural practice that can only feed the country with no surplus is still at a subsistence level of agriculture. Agricultural industry will be developed when the small-scale farmers are helped to perform. The farmers will specialize in the areas of their production and there will be surplus products. Large-scale farmers are productive, but they are so few that their production will not satisfactorily help the economy of the nation. Farming is difficult and unpredictable. It is not easy to aspire to large-scale farming. But a small-scale farmer is sure of production, and if encouraged and helped, he will be sure to produce more.

Government assistance is helpful but government participation is dangerous to the farming industry. Agriculture needs a direct attachment. It does not need indirect attention. Agriculture wants owner participation so as to be able to make immediate decisions in delicate matters. The direct attachment in agriculture makes a farmer work on a "timeless watch." A farmer does not watch his watch while on the farm.

This is one of the weaknesses of large-scale farming. As the farm grows, the large-scale is detached from the direct touch of its owner. Although he may be productive, the small-scale farmer is more efficient. The agricultural revolution will begin with developing the available indigenous crops and materials. Agricultural revolution is not importing modern technologies from outside the country. It is improving the indigenous *cultures* within the country. This should be done by the use of common resources. Scarce resources will not create revolution because they cannot be easily available. I give full example of what I mean by revolution with indigenous resources. In Nigeria water and temperature are common resources which can be easily used for agricultural revolution. Nigeria has good temperatures which allow crops to grow all year round, but Nigeria has no year-round rainfall. Rain pours only during the rainy season. When the flood water is captured by constructing simple artificial dams, it can be used for irrigation during the dry season. This results in continuous planting and continuous harvesting. If the crop is vegetables, there will be surplus vegetables all the year round. Any industry based on vegetables will not lack raw materials because the production is based on the available common resources. This simple revolution will create a chain of revolution. There will be a solution of idle labour because the continuity of production will bring stability of income for the people in that area. There will be a good network of roads because the floods which destroy the roads are redirected away from the road system to agrarian production. There are similar revolutions in many areas. Thinking big and high is not economic development. Economic development is revolution from below. There are stages which will be followed from below. Not until such stages are followed will the economy be developed. Imitations and gigantic plans cannot do it. That is what this book is trying to prove.

# Chapter 6
# Cottage Industry

The surplus from developed agriculture is food elements. It is raw material. So there is need to deal with the surplus food to avoid spoilage. There are three basic ways of food preservation:

1. Canning
2. Drying
3. Freezing

These are the functions of cottage industries. These industries spring up in many places to take care of the surplus food elements. There is specialization in cottage industry depending upon the kind of crops raised in an area. Cottage industry is the first step to manufacturing industry. Cottage industry tried to turn raw foods into a finished product that is ready to serve. Or it may preserve the raw food for future usage. Cottage industries help to train a country to go into giant industries. While practicing cottage industries the people will pass through many disappointments. Efforts to solve these disappointments will help in acquiring the knowledge that builds the large-scale industries which have complex structures. It is not feasible for a nation to escape cottage industry which is the early development of industrial revolution, and be able to practice large-scale industries successfully. One aspect of simple cottage industry is that it affords an understanding and impetus that help in unity of practice. For a successful large-scale complex industry there must be a unity of action. When the simple cottage industries realize that they cannot perform efficiently in all the areas of complex industries, they will unite for efficient performance in all the areas of large-scale industry. The knowhows derived from the cottage industries will be used to build large-scale industries. The unity is forced due to the hardships experienced in practicing alone.

## Transportation and Communication

Cottage industry can take place in rural areas where there is no adequate transportation because cottage industry uses raw materials located in the areas of their production. But it may not exhaust all the raw materials. Some of the products of cottage industry may be an input to other industries. The remaining raw materials not used by the cottage industry may be needed in other places. Market is created for utilization of the surplus raw products and the cottage industry products. The transportation system is built to help deliver the products. One of the reasons division of labour and specialization is lacking in developing countries is due to inadequate transportation system. The agricultural products are lumped in the areas of production with no way of sending them to the areas needing them. Also many areas may need the supply of an output of an industry for an input for its production. But since there is no transportation system to send the required input to the area involved, the producer tries to produce the required materials for their industries. For example, in the poultry industry a poultry farmer who wants to be successful would be required to produce all the necessary materials to run the industry. He produces corn, feed, hatchery, and the rest. If there is specialization of all the sectors of the poultry industry, and a good transportation system, a poultry farmer could specialize in one area of poultry industrial production like egg production, table chicken production, or others. A good transportation system helps make materials available for the production of goods.

A transportation system is meaningless if there is no network of roads. Without a good road system, the rest of the developments will not take place. Water, electricity, and the rest follow the roads.

The trucking industry will be developed as a result of the road system. The problem of bottlenecks in economic production would be solved. Raw materials will be taken to the areas where they are needed, and finished products will be taken to the markets. The collection industry will collect from the small producers and small buyers and take the goods to the storage industry.

## Storage

The developing countries think of agriculture in its subsistence level of operation. People are limited to one kind of action, and they do everything from production to marketing. Developed agriculture needs division of work and specialization. There are many promising areas of business in agriculture. The trucking industry is one of the areas. Storage is another area. In order to be able to develop stable manufacturing industries, there will be a storage system whereby raw materials are stored and whereby finished products are also stored. The storage goes with collection. Many small buyers will sell to the storage industry where preservation and storage are done. The storage industry will undertake supplying the manufacturers through the trucking industry. These systems give a continuity of supply to the manufacturers. There will be stability in the economy. Each area produces what it is required to produce, and what it produces can be found at any time by the industry using it. Storage becomes the centre of collection and distribution of materials both for production and for consumption.

## Consumption

When production and distribution are discussed as an aid to development, consumption will be dealt with because it is the end of distribution, and it has great impact on development. We always say that the consumer is king. Consumption is very impportant in the economy. It creates demand for a commodity. Demand generates the supply of the commodity. When there is increase in supply it means that production is increased. Increase in production due to consumption means that the economy is developing.

Consumption will also destroy production. Conspicuous consumption destroys the incentive to produce a certain product, mostly indigenous products. But it increases the production of foreign goods that are consumed. Gluttony also disturbs production by exhausting the income that would go to saving and investment. A worker who spends all his wages cannot save. He will not be able to progress. A nation that consumes all her production cannot save and cannot invest and, therefore, can never industrialize. There is a system of forced saving whereby a policy is made to induce food out of gluttonous mouths. This is done by pricing. Manufacturers offer more money to the food producers and this will help in collection and storage of raw materials for industry. Actually one of the signs of development is the ability to sacrifice luxurious items and pay more attention to investment items. When people's propensity to save increases, investment must likewise increase, thus development increases.

## Division of Labour and Specialization

"Jack of all trade is the master of none," and "Rolling stone collects no moss." No mortal body can be ubiquitous. Ubiquity is for the spirits. No one can be efficient in all areas. Efficiency in a system will be achieved when experts are located in the areas of their specialities. All economic resources are limited—labour, knowledge, crops, money, and so on. These can never be produced by a person or group of people alone. Therefore division of labour is employed to make someone or some group of people be responsible in producing what they are able to produce with the least cost of materials and the least cost of time. Specialization is employed to make people undertake production in areas in which they have the advantage of knowhow. Advantage relates to knowledge, interest, and resource availability. Those who have the advantage in land specialize in crops. Those who have the advantage in warehouses and big stores go into storage. Those who have small trucks, bicycles, and strength to carry specialize in the collection industry. Where a country does not divide and specialize, there will be no stable production and no efficiency. Dynamic social development encourages the division of labour and specialization. For example a knowledge of soil conditions in Nigeria will help in locating a yam belt, corn belt, cocoa belt, etc. These areas with their different soil advantages will be made to raise what they have the advantage in raising. Our biggest problem is finding where the money comes from easily. There is no way one can find easy money. Most economic "windfall" wealth is due to great persistency in a field or a business. Division of labour and specialization can occur in all areas of economy. Service industries will produce services. Their products will be purchased and from that they buy other consumables. If a service industry is involved in other forms of production, there must be a conflict of interest and inefficiency. Farmers will produce food for the consumption of the people and industries and surplus for exports. If farmers are involved in other forms of business there will be a conflict of interest and inefficiency. Manufacturers will produce goods for people to consume and surplus for export. If they are involved in other forms of business, there will be a conflict of interest and inefficiency. The conflicts of interest in Nigeria are the deficiencies in the Nigerian economy.

Some time is spent in private practices and some revenue goes to the private sector which would have gone to the public sector. Conflict of interest will be more in citizen farming when it is fully practiced.

These conflicts are due to lack of division of labour and specialization. We want money by any means in any way. But we cannot find stable money in that way. Division of labour and specialization bring stability in a country's economy and in the country itself.

# Chapter 7

# Savings, Investment, and Employment

## Savings and Investment

Developing countries have low income per capita, yet they will be praised for their efforts in saving and investment. During the subsistence level of economy the developing countries organized forced savings whereby some of their small incomes were saved. These organizations are given different names: susu, contribution, meeting, trade association, and so on. The system is to make small money contributions to one person who wants to embark on an investment project. The money so collected will be invested in the project. Formerly the banking system did not make money available to the indigenous business people in developing countries because of the instability of the economic system in these countries. The developing countries made impressive efforts and defeated the policy of the banking system. These associations that finance investment projects in the developing countries so organize themselves that the contribution money was the first priority in their household budget. The remainder, after the deduction of the contribution money, would go into consumption:

Income = Contribution plus Consumption
Contribution = Income minus Consumption
Savings = Income minus Consumption

Therefore Contribution = Saving.

The meeting members must see that the intended contribution must be used for the intended goal. The intended goal would be of investment nature. The example of the goal would be buying a vehicle, or marrying a wife, or paying school fees for the children. So contribution is saving and saving is investment.

In discussing the real takeoff in the money economy in developing countries, it must be noted that the contribution money is responsible for most of the investments made in these countries. There is need to define investment in relation to the developing countries. Investment is expenditure made in any project which has no immediate consumption effort. For example, buying vehicles for the performance of jobs, paying money for apprentice contracts, paying school fees, building homes, purchase of land, and starting petty trade. These were among the ends that the contributions served. These made the real foundation of the big projects in developing countries.

## Employment

Social development has many approaches. Let us look at them in purely economic terms and try to explore how they will aid development.

Employment generates production in the economy. In a country with a high unemployment rate the economy is in big trouble. But employment will be based on the availability of funds to pay the labour. When we think about employment in developing countries we think about the government as an employer. This is the mistake. In any country employment is the function of both the public sector and the private sector. Public employment produces services. Since the gross national product is comprised of goods and services, and since the private sector produces goods, private employment helps more in increasing the GNP of a country. It is difficult to introduce private employment in a backward country because of selfish philosophy. The attitude towards wealth is that of accumulation for selfish ends and not that of generating employment. There is a tendency to brood over possessions. One person tries to do what many people should do. The person does that so as to realize the whole profit of the enterprise. Division of labour and specialization help to create employment in the areas where labour is specialized. There are many real estate owners without rent collectors, janitors, and yard cleaners. There are many shops without clerks. There are many motor transport owners who have only a driver to work on the transport. Touts each collect about thirty to fifty naira daily from the motor transport sector. But this money is unaccounted for and, therefore, not taxed. Since it is difficult to abolish touts, I suggest that they be legalized and registered so as to collect taxes from them according to their income.

In the public employment system, the investigation of "ghost workers" by the government revealed that some senior people take the salaries of the ghost workers. Some workers do not give their full services to the government. They give government half and give half to their private practices. All these are services that would have generated more employment if they were honestly and properly utilized. Well supervised employment generates more employment. For a takeoff in economic development the idle labours and resources will be employed. This will be done by the private and public sectors. The private sector will give employment in real estate management, private stores and shops, cottage industries, and farms. The public sector will create employment in the areas much needed by the labour force.

Since capital is essential in production and employment, the private sector, in order to be able to generate saving, finds ways to thrift. The consumption that is not made becomes the savings of the people. These savings are the capital which is invested in many ways. Employment is made and production increases.

## Labour/Capital Function

The profit maximization aims at the least cost production. Production is the function of labour and capital. A unit of output is produced by the combination of labour and capital. If a hundred units of output is produced by the use of ten labour and five capital, and if by more use of labour and less use of capital—say, twelve labour and four capital—the same hundred units of output is produced. But labour costs much more than capital. In order to maximize profit, more capital and less labour is used. But in the developing countries there is more labour than capital. The employment of more capital so as to maximize profit creates another problem of displaced labour. The dynamic social development tries to point out most of the problems experienced by the early social development of the Western nations so as to check them and have a stable development in developing countries. One of the problems of developing countries is that the nation does not care for the people. It was like this in the development of the Western nations. The land enclosures and the capital introduction displaced the labour and pushed the labour out of the country to the cities. The influx of labour to the cities created a lot of problems which they struggled to solve all through their development period. The diseases, early deaths, dehumanization of people, and abuses of woman and child labour were among the problems experienced by the Western nations in their development. This was why Marx, Engels, Veblen and other social reformers came into prominence. The developing countries will be in a better position if they look into labour-capital functions at this initial stage, and try to regulate it to protect labour and develop according to the labour-capital ratio. When labour decreases capital will be much used, and in areas where labour cannot perform, capital will be used. The word capital includes all the rest of the production elements including equipment. Only human labour is left. The present system will be labour intensive. This will employ most of the labour and avoid economic waste due to idle labour. The truth is that idle labour must eat and live like any human being. The more idle labour increases, the more food shortage there will be. The more idle labour is not employed the more the country is on the verge of trouble. *Towards a Dynamic Social Development* recommends decentralization of the economic development scheme so as to tie the country labour in country places.

# Chapter 8

## Development Location, Liquid Capital and Market Development Location

Developing countries interfere with the economic development in such a way that hinders development. There is a high degree of commitment and interest in economic development projects. The commitment and interest make any person involved in it persist in the midst of difficulties. The presence of abandoned development projects is a proof of lack of attention and interest. Economic development is the function of the local governments and people. This allows the local government areas to embark on the project in their interest utilizing their availability of resources. But if the state and federal government direct economic development projects, there will be a tendency to locate wrong development projects in some areas. The political actors will try to locate projects to their areas not on the basis of procurring required resources, but on the basis of power struggle. Any successful development project must be the project owned by the interested persons and located in the areas where the project development input is available.

Priorities are essential in economic development. But priorities depend upon the project goal and resources availability. Any area will base its priority on the kind of project it wants. However there are general priorities to economic development projects. A road system is the first aspect of development to be undertaken. Roads should be constructed to important places to give access to movement of people and materials needed for any kind of project. The location of a development project depends on the area where water is available. So water helps in locating development projects. It may be a stream, river, lake, or good reliable tap water system. The third project is electricity. There is need for power to be able to process the raw products into manufactured products. The government will help in road, water, and electricity. The people will make use of the available resources in their area and develop the project required according to the supply of advantaged resources.

## Liquid Capital

Developing countries have problems with liquidity. When will circulating money be increased in a country? How will inflation be controlled? Will the government print money as the population increases? Or will the government print money when she needs the money?

The approach to these questions will begin with production. The government's function is to purchase the goods and the services produced by the people. The government purchases services through employment, but how she purchases the goods is another question. Assume that a small country produced ten million tons of corn last year, and this year the country produced fifteen million tons. The ten million tons of corn cost four million naira. When there is increase of corn production by five million tons, the government will do something to clear the five million tons from the market. The increase is the additional money that will go into circulation. If the money is not made available to clear the excess production, the value of corn drops. This is analysis for home market. But internationally the currency of a nation rules in that nation. An average Nigerian woman in a home local market does not know what a dollar is just as an average American woman in the United States of America does not know what a naira is. But they know and enjoy the products of one another's nation. So the national currency is backed by the productivity of these nations. Trade is the exchange of home products for imported products. So when Nigerian goods that are sold in the U.S.A. increases, it means that Nigerian foreign exchange increases. So also the U.S.A. products in Nigeria increase as the U.S. foreign exchange increases. But if Nigeria does not sell her products to the outside world and she continues consuming the products from the other countries, her balance of trade will be very poor. This imbalance of trade is what Nigeria suffers because she consumes other products not producing her own to balance it. The imbalance of trade is an ill wind. It does not favour any country. Any country that exports and does not import will be in difficulty with her balance of trade. But any country struggles to export more than she imports because that will give her a favourable balance of trade. As John Stuart Mill puts it, "The values at which a country exchanges its produce with foreign countries depend on the amount and extensibility of their demand for its demand for theirs. The more the foreign demand for its commodities exceeds demand for foreign commodities the more favourable to it will be the terms of exchange; that is, the more it will obtain of foreign commodities in return for a given quantity of its own."[9]

From these analyses we will agree that the productivity of a country controls a country's currency. When the home production increases, the home currency in circulation increases. When the export production increases, the foreign exchange increases. Nigeria's article of foreign trade is petroleum. The demand for this alone will determine the treat-

9. John Stuart Mill, *Principles of Political Economy* (London: Longmans Green and Co., 1920), 603.

ment Nigeria gets in terms of exchanging for foreign commodities. If there is any problem with the petroleum price, it will have an adverse effect on the Nigerian economy. Nigeria has no other export product, but Nigeria imports nearly everything she needs in her country. The import and export cannot balance with only one export product. There is much foreign exchange needed to balance the deficits created by the huge consumption of imported goods. The necessary condition for a dynamic economic development is dynamic social change to embrace all areas of social phenomena. It will be cultural development of all social phenomena. Imitation of foreign culture is not dynamic change because it is not from within the society. The dynamic social change is the kind of change that can compete with foreign culture. If it is a product it will compete favourably with foreign products on the open market. A country's cultural product is a product originated from the country. Such products have the power of competition and can generate demand for the country's culture. The cultural products can be imitated, but the imitation cannot be the actuality.

## Market

In developing countries the market is a free market. The definition of a market in developing countries is a place where commodities are assembled for people to buy and sell. No one controls it. This is why pricing is not steady. The buyer and the seller bargain until the agreed price is reached. The price works with the commodities and controls the commodities. When there are many commodities the price will go down, but if the commodities are few the price will go up. The market is also a place where the people meet for certain rituals. It is a place where friends meet to visit after days of work. It is a place of rest and worship. The market is a place where certain funeral functions are performed. It is held on selected days. It serves as a place to disseminate information. It is a place of actions for developing countries. It is a place of rest and worship. So it is located near a religious shrine or a central place for the whole community. The size depends upon the amount of the commodities and what the community can produce. Where there are many agricultural products, the market is very big. The social development in the market begins with making the marketplace a daily market. The size will be enlarged and people will build a living quarters around it. The stores will be erected and more commodities sent from other places. The stores will sell manufactured products which can be stored for a long time without spoiling. Roads will be constructed to carry commodities to and from the market.

## Supply and Demand and Price

Supply and demand depend upon the existence of a commodity. People demand what they see, that is, what exists. If a commodity does not exist, nobody will demand it. So the first demand people made was for agricultural products. The fruits, leaves, roots, and live stock meat were what people saw and demanded in primitive economy. The trade was by barter. The exchange by barter depended upon quantity in the market. If there were more yams and less corn, many yams would buy few corn. The quantity worked with exchange rate.

The demand for manufactured goods was due to presentation of these goods to the developing countries. The problem of development began with the action of developed countries. The developing countries could produce the agricultural products because they saw them and demanded them. But manufactured goods were presented to the developing countries for consumption only. The developing countries did not see where they were made and how they were made. The problem of development was educating people to consume and not educating them to produce. The law of demand and supply in developing countries was greatly limited, and it was a partial law with the undeveloped economy. The agricultural commodities spoil, they are bulky, there is no space to store them. The care for the commodities controls the accumulation and demand of the products. But the developed economy has no demand limitation. The manufactured products can remain for years, some thousand naira products can be packed in a briefcase, and above all, the invention of monetary system and banking process make people's wants insatiable. With high demand of good not produced in developing countries and with the supply from outside the countries, the price becomes uncontrollable in developing countries' markets. The free market is distorted. The developing countries adhere to the policy of protectionism, and developed countries pursue the policy of exploitation through the free market system. That is, the developing countries try to protect their economy so as to be able to develop manufacturing of their goods. The developed countries spoil the developing countries' economy by pushing more of the manufactured goods into the developing countries. The sign of development is the ability of the developing countries to grasp the situation and change and concentrate on the development of their own culture. Dynamic social change begins with the change of mind in developing countries. Such change will affect consumption; conspicuous consumption will stop. The change will encourage cultural production of the products of developing countries.

# Chapter 9
# Economic Policy and Social Utility

## Policy

Policy rules any society. Any disturbance in a society will be traced from the policy that rules the society. It may be that the people do not obey the policy or it may be that the policy itself is wrong. Policy is made for the whole society. When there is a partial observation of a policy, the enforcement of that policy becomes difficult and the policy ceases to work.

Policy helps in the development of a country. Any country makes her policy in the direction of the development she wants. The country uses the organs of policy to direct the people to the area she wants the people to go. The fiscal policy helps in the allocation of resources and collection of revenue. The economic policy helps in the production and consumption behaviour of the people. The tariff policy helps in the export and import of the goods to be used in the country or the goods to be exported to other countries. With a good policy the people are made to do anything they are asked to do in a peaceful way. For example, the United States of America has a policy of separation of church and state. The state will never help the church financially but there is a policy whereby the people are made to help the church. The church is a nonprofit organization and there is a policy of claiming any amount given to the church as a tax free gift and deductible on one's income tax. This makes many people give to the church of their choice to support it.

In developing African and Asian countries the problem is making policies that cannot work. Any policy that is made must be observed by all the people both nationals and aliens in a country. If a policy is made and certain individuals think themselves excluded from the policy, that policy will not work. A country will produce what she wants her citizens to consume. There is no need of a policy telling the citizens to consume indigenous products where there are not enough indigenous products. Any imported product to be consumed in a country will not have a restricted import license. It will have an open import licence or government controlled importation. The preferential import licence enriches certain people and encourages uncontrolled inflation. Public properties will be used for public goals and not redirected to private goals. If this policy is observed by all the citizens, public properties will not be abused.

The policy control of one area of business will make the resources be redirected to other areas. For example if real estate property is restricted to only one plot or two for a person in any city of Nigeria and not more than one city, there will be redirection of resources to other areas of development. Industrial development, agricultural development, and rural areas will have attention. Those who have will think of other areas in which to invest their resources. Real estate ownership is eroding developing countries resources and other areas are neglected.

## Fiscal Policy

The slogan of no taxation without representation still holds up. The representation in taxation is the census. No tax will be efficient if the census of the country and incomes of the people are not known. The beginning of efficiency in taxation is the knowledge of the census of the nation. The tax census is not head count census. Registration census is more efficient than head count census. In developing nations where extended relationship is so strong registration census will be very possible. The registration census will help in the knowledge of the estimate of income of a person. Ability to pay will be determined from that, and collection will depend on the area of operation and registration. The registration will help to know about the aliens in the country, and population of the country will be easily estimated.

The efficiency in fiscal policy and government spending will help to develop a built-in stabilizer which helps in solution of economic instability. The problem with developing countries is that these countries are influenced by wrong methods of application of good policies. The reason is that developing countries like to employ their relatives or friends in vacant posts. This destroys efficiency. There is no problem in employing a Nigerian in a post whether relative or not. The problem is employing a wrong person to a post. These are economic wastes. The developing countries employ not on the basis of knowhow or capability to perform, but on the basis of earning one's livelihood. This is why they want relatives to earn their livelihood. This is not a good qualification for the national interest. The national interest in employment is a good performance from the nationals no matter who performs. There is another observed fact with the politicians. They like to employ foreigners or people who would hide their selfish ends. They do not like to employ an honest person who would expose their selfish intentions. The people they so recruited would be pursuing their own selfish interests while maintaining their employer's selfish interests.

## Social Utility or Development Utility

The concept of utility in economics is attributed to the mind of an individual in want of satisfaction. This is derived through individual tastes and enjoyments. Social utility is the satisfaction derived from the social consumption. It is the social satisfaction because the society consumes it. It is the satisfaction derived from the consumption which another person makes. Social utility is development utility. It is the enjoyment we have in development or living in developed society. Social consumption is included in individual consumption. An individual can have a satisfaction from a cup of water by drinking it himself. Totality of such satisfaction is social satisfaction. Individuals cannot have a satisfaction from the telephone by using it alone, having no other person at the other end. Society will have social satisfaction from tap water running in their community, from a telephone system and a road system in their area. These explain social consumption. This is the satisfaction one has because one shares their own satisfaction with others. The concept of development utility helps to realize the reason why development should be the involvement of the society. No selfish person can have and enjoy it alone. This is the reason why after building a mansion with electricity and water in a rural place, the person still lives in an undeveloped place. It is so because the enjoyment is centered on one's family. When the enjoyment is generally distributed to the whole society it gives social satisfaction. This satisfaction is derived in the establishment of many social and public amenities. Some people refuse to repair their road in rural places simply because they have no cars. Such reasoning shows lack of the knowledge of development utility. The social consumption of roads is that a friend or someone else visits his friend or someone else undisturbed.

## Total Development Utility (TUD)

Total development utility is the summation of the utilities derived from development facilities. They are easy communications, clean society, good sanitation, good water supply and good roads.

## Marginal Utility of Development (MUD)

Marginal social utility is the utility derived from additional units of development. That is, total social utility minus the total utility of development less one i.e., MUD = TUD - TUD - 1. Let us assume that the total development utility is road, water, electricity and telephone. The marginal utility of development is road, water, electricity and telephone minus road, water and electricity. The additional unit of development is telephone.

## Assume Fixed Input and Two Variables

The fixed input is the town. The two variables are road and water. When the construction and fittings are going on, the people are happy although they have not started using them. The happiness increases as the work progresses. When the work is completed and the people begin to use the road and enjoy the good water supply, any attempt to extend the road or the water will be disutility of development because that extention would destroy farms or useful structures and people will kick against it.

## Assume All Input Variables

There is room for expansion so no input is fixed. Social utility will have no maximum. Any input gives increasing expansion and increasing utility. The marginal utility of development cannot be satisfied. Development like civilization has rooms for expansion, and it is impossible to attain full civilization or full development. Since there is room for expansion, there is room for utility. There are damaged and unmaintained roads, there are broken water pipes, there are beggars in the streets, there is unemployment all over the country and there are robbers harassing the people. All these bring unhappiness to people which results in the disutility of development. But when they are treated, utility increases. It is very difficult for a sincere citizen to have full happiness and social satisfaction when other members of the society are in pain or live in pitiful condition. Although amenities give social satisfaction, these pitiful conditions give social dissatisfaction. Only sadists will be happy with the bad conditions of others.

## Total Social Utility

*A* is stage one of social utility. The people are anxious to see the improvement of their area and they expect social consumption.

*B* is stage two of social utility. Work is in progress to the point that some people are enjoying amenities. At the maximum point all people enjoy these amenities.

*C* is stage three of social utility. Any additional unit of social utility to the fixed input will create a problem and not happiness.

## All Inputs are Variable

a = The decreasing utility due to wear and tear or destruction of amenities.

b = The increasing utility due to repair and expansion of amenities.

## Total Social Utility

(*Fixed inputs and two variable inputs.*)

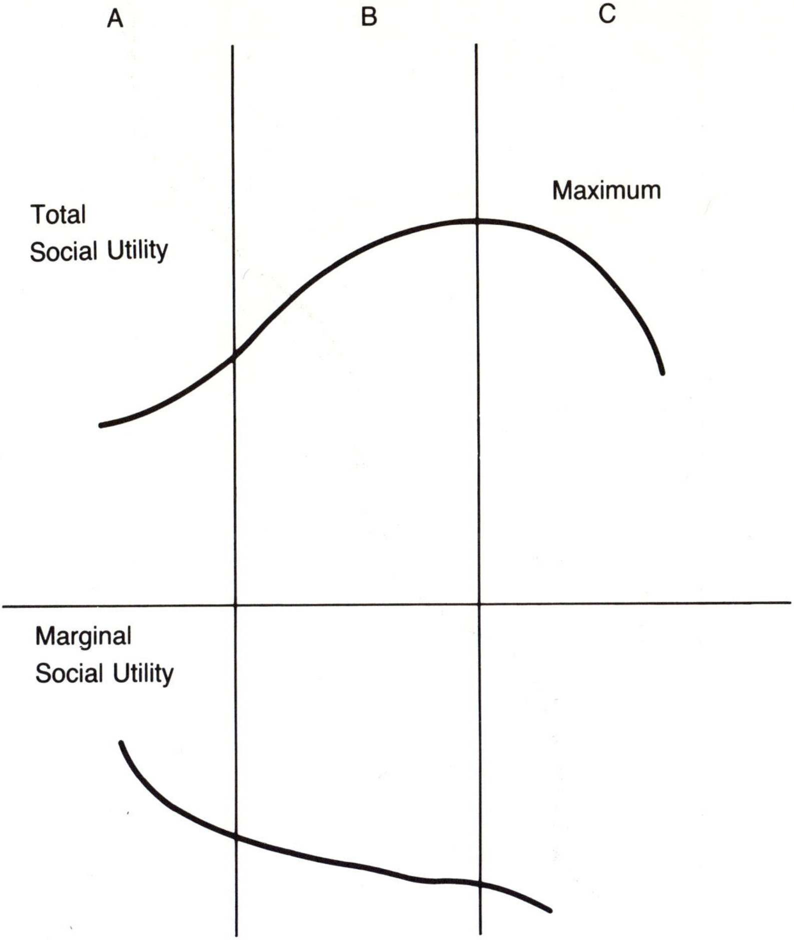

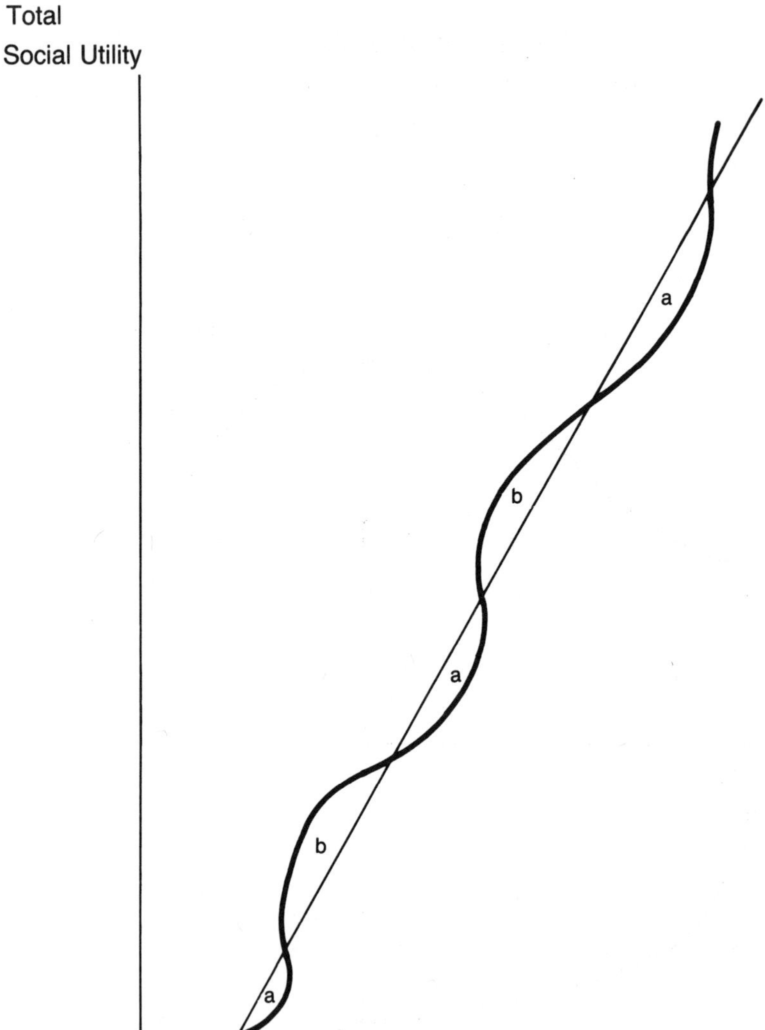
Total
Social Utility
a
b
a
b
a

# Part III
# Political Development

# Chapter 10

## Development of Nigerian Nation and Checks and Balances

David Easton said that politics is the allocator of all values. However strong and whatever incentive the people have, whatever resources there are in a nation, the future and the hope of the nation is in the hands of its political body. They can make or unmake a nation. Sometimes they are aware of it; sometimes they may not know what they are doing, but it happens.

Like any development, political development will begin somewhere very near to scratch. Economic development started from the application of indigenous knowledge to indigenous materials to create homemade cultures or products. Development of politics will begin with the application of indigenous knowledge to indigenous cultures. Since culture is built around religion, the development of a political cultural pattern will borrow its format from religion. The religion of any nation is nationalism, where this is lacking there is no nation. Political development is therefore the development of nationalism. The responsibility of political development is to tie the religious and cultural differences in a country together to form a national culture. This system when developed will tie the citizens together and there will be unity. The unity of the people becomes the nation. Nationalism in European countries can be different from the nationalism in African countries. The differences lie in the cultures of these countries on which their nationalism is built. But all the nationalisms have the same function to perform, i.e. the protection of the interests of the nation, and bringing unity and stability to the nation.

## Nigerian Nation

Nigeria will achieve in time a nationhood when there is development of national culture. The national culture will serve the state, tribes, and religions in Nigeria. This national culture must be respected by all the people in Nigeria, both citizens and aliens. No state, tribe, or sectional culture will have conflict with the Nigerian national culture. The national culture will be involved with the preservation of human life, human dignity, and human freedom—that is freedom of worship, freedom of speech, and freedom of movement.

Freedom of worship means that Nigerians will not be molested for any right belief. Right belief will satisfy the wishes of the Nigerian nation. Where religion preaches hatred and disunity it does not satisfy the wishes of the people of Nigeria. Separation of church and state means that no religious affairs will be enforced on the state. No state revenue will go directly or indirectly to any religion. One's religion is one's responsibility and not a state responsibility. For example, there were two visits of religious heads from outside countries into Nigeria. By separation of church and state there would be no state reception for any church leader. The church leaders would be received by their church members and friends. No state representative will go to the reception on behalf of the state, but a government man can go as a member of a church or as a friend. This will make the Nigerian nation uncommitted and unbiased. National culture will superimpose tribal and religious cultures. National cultures will tie Nigerians together under the name of Nigeria. (This will be discussed more in nationalism under philosophy and religion.)

Religion and age form the political control in primitive society. The development of a nation will be the transference of the allegiance from the aged people, and religious heads to the nation. The people will look upon the nation as they look upon their old people and religious heads. They will respect the nation as they respect the religious leaders and old people. The nation will be the central focus of cultures and ideas and will attract the whole people. Age and religion will be respected because they are merged to the central culture. The tribal religions and cultures will stop dominating the people because their leaders have jointly transferred their allegiances to the nation. All unite to form a national culture. Nigeria will have the standard national culture that all the citizens will observe and defend. The difficulty now is that the tribal leaders hold to their tribes and serve the interest of their tribes. When they transfer these services to the nation, their supporters will look upon the nation as the one and only identity of the whole people. Nigeria will be a nation and serve her people as one nation.

To paraphrase the late Dr. Martin Luther King Jr., Nigerians will live together like brothers and sisters in a united Nigeria or they will perish together like fools in a divided Nigeria.

## Political Checks and Balances

Cultural observation shows that primitive people have means of disciplining the society. Norms, mores, and oaths are the observed means of checking the people from misbehaving. Via norms and mores people have standard and ideal ways of action. People act under the control of the cultural standard of the people. For political stability, the political actors must be checked when they perform in the public offices, and the public must be checked to see that they are in line with the public policies and goals. Political checks and balances begin with the way the political actors are brought into power. Where this fails to function properly there will be instability. The system of election, if followed properly, will bring peace. But where the system fails to work there must be another measure to correct it. When a nation devises methods of correcting the abuses or wrong behaviors of the people, the nation will be stable. For a political development to be stable there must be checks to abuses introduced in the system so as to bring balance in the system.

The system of political checks can be in the following forms.

1. *The voting system*: Voting system is where the citizens vote a person of their choice into political offices. The voting system makes the candidates behave so as to be able to impress the future voters.
2. *Law-enforcement officers*: Police and other law enforcement officers are the officers of social checks. The presence of police in a place means absence of abuses. So wherever they are, there must be checks to any abuse. Where this fails to work in this way, there is social disaster.
3. *Judicial system*: The judicial system checks the behaviour of the people. Since all citizens are liable to court procedure and are liable to punishment when they are found guilty, they will behave to free themselves from court actions.
4. *Public opinion*: Public opinion expressed in the news media checks the evil doers because nobody likes to be exposed to the public in a derogatory manner.

5. *Constitution*: The Constitution of the nation spells out the relationships between the government and the people, between people and people, and between the states and central government. It also spells out the limits of performance of political actors and the time of changes. No one person dominates the offices.
6. *Military intervention*: Military intervention is a check to political leaders when the political leaders abuse their offices and become very strong and powerful, so that when the public and the law enforcement agencies cannot check them, the military will. The history of political development reveals that some of the developed nations passed through a series of military interventions. Military intervention is a conventional intervention where and when all the powers of checks and balances have failed. But maturity in political development develops correcting actions so as to avoid military interventions.

# Chapter 11
# Social Change

Social change is a change of cultural pattern. It may be the improvement of the existing culture. Or it may remove the existing culture and introduce another. But whatever direction a social change takes, there must be an element of cultural continuity which will give it the name of what it is: the cultural product of the producers. There are obstacles to social change. A change is the growing awareness of the present condition and readiness to accept another condition. No society can change if their minds are not ready to move away from the old system. Social change can be categorized in these steps.

Step 1: There is a growing dissatisfaction in the society. There are other conditions elsewhere better than the conditions within the society. People are frustrated and want to enjoy such conditions in their country.

Step 2: The ways of bringing social enjoyment into the society:

I. By importation of the amenities: If there is easy importation of social amenities, the people will import them and enjoy them. There will be no effort to produce them at home. The easy acquisition of enjoyments will disturb development. No incentive to produce the amenities will be developed. The import business and the distribution of the enjoyment facilities will form the major businesses in the area.

II. Difficult import policy: Where the enjoyable things are not easy to obtain, the people will do all they can to produce them at home. If the policy is favourable to production development, the country will develop the production of the new products locally. The society will be developed.

III. Iron curtain laws: Where the new products are not easy to obtain, and the policy is not favourable to develop the new products at home. The people's desire to produce the new products will be obstructed by these rigid policies. The people will be entrenched in the old method because of fear. Their minds will never move towards inventive attitudes. In such conditions it is very difficult to accept change, and development is difficult. Whenever there are any new conditions the dominant factors for change are:

A. The attitude of the people to consumption.

B. The policies governing the people and consumption of goods.

C. The attitude of the people to the policies.

Step 3. Conflict of cultures: when there is meeting of two phenomena there will be a crash or explosion. For example, the meeting of two winds results in thunder and lightning, the meeting of two rivers or water channels results in rapids or storms. The meeting of two cultures brings misunderstanding and social disturbance. The meeting of the philosophy of Christ and the philosophy of Judaism brought lots of problems in the time of Christ. Today the philosophy of colonialism and the philosophy of independence must bring social disturbance when they meet. The two cultures will not agree. This is one of the experiences of the new nations. The problem is how to reconcile the old and new philosophies. Christ said that when a person with evil spirit was freed from the evil spirit, the place was left unoccupied. When that evil spirit found that the place was unoccupied, it would take the evil spirit worse than itself, and enter into that person, and his condition would be worse then before. The interpretation is that when the evil spirit was forced out, the person would receive the spirit of God so that when another evil spirit came, it would see that the place was occupied. This can be attributed to new nations. The exodus of the colonial power left the independent countries with a vacuum. The colonial system which the occupied countries were complaining about was removed. The old methods and colonial exploitations were removed. The countries became empty of philosophic system. Then neocolonialism entered into the countries and their conditions became worse than before. The exploiters now became difficult to purge because they have roots in the countries they exploit. They are part of the system that exploits the system. The dynamic social change maintains that colonial exploitation will be replaced with honest and hard work, that is, colonialism will be replaced with nationalism. Sectionalism and tribalism will be replaced with unity and peace. These are the roots of development.

Most leaders in developing countries do not like to make names. They like to make wealth. This attitude leads to the foundation of selfishness and dishonesty. In any nation where the people are bent towards subjectivity, the building of philosophic schools is not possible. Philosophic schools are the results of objective thinkers. Hence Marx said, "No society can last long unless it provides for the motives of diverse personalities; and no philosophic system can have a universal appeal unless it incorporates the most contrary themes. A consistent philosophy can never have more than a secretarian following."[10]

10. Marx and Engels, xi.

No philosophy can affiliate itself with another philosophy. If it tries to do so, the two philosophies will crumble. But a philosophy can be developed from the originality of thinking of its founder. No new wine can be put in an old wine skin, and no old cloth can be sewn to a new cloth. If such is done it must end in ruin. Old wine must be in old wine skins, and new wine in new wine skins. Likewise old cloth will be patched with the old cloth and new cloth will be patched with new cloth.

A dynamic social change must have its original philosophy backed by its indigenous culture. No imitation will be a dynamic social change because it cannot stay. A dynamic social change has its own life, the life which started at its birthplace and developed there. Dynamic social change has its roots—unity, honesty, and peace. This is discussed in another section.

# Chapter 12
# Politics and Morality

There are phenomena that disturb development but they are not discussed in development. These phenomena will be discussed here. They are rights, privileges, and political morality.

## Rights

Individual rights of a citizen have many ways of being interpreted. They may mean rights of existence in one's country. They may be equal opportunity rights. They may mean rights to one's property. They may mean rights to freedom of speech and religious freedom. Whatever rights we claim, the correct right is right to do the right thing in one's country. If one does the wrong thing in one's country one's rights will be denied to him or her. The question is what is the right thing in one's country? The answer is the national interest of a country is the right thing any person in a country should pursue, whether a citizen of the country or an alien in the country. The national interest is spelled out in the constitution and laws or decrees of a country. A person's life may be denied him or her if the person commits an offence that warrants execution. A person's property will be confiscated if it is proved that the property is acquired illegally. The rights of a citizen will be maintained when the citizen pursues a life that helps in development of his or her country: honest work in office, consumption of goods manufactured in the country, the avoidances of importation of contraband goods, respecting the rights of others, and the policies and laws of the country. Many people claim wrong things to be right. For example, Nigerian property rights are wrongly claimed. In any landed property there are sections that are owned by the public. These sections are used for the public utilities' connections. But property owners wall around all the property areas so that there is no room for public utilities' connections. Also along the streets and market squares people display their merchandise and deny others the use of the public places. These people claim the right to do so not knowing that they are wrong because they deny others the use of the public space. A good education on the rights of the citizen will help in having a steady, stable, dynamic development. A person who wants to grab the public resources to enrich himself is not doing the right thing. The knowledge of the rights of a citizen will help in knowing how to care for public resources. It is not right to cheat a person or the public. We will respect the rights of others and the public. When we deny others' rights or deny public's rights, we abuse our own rights, and our rights will be denied us. We have responsible right and not absolute or irresponsible right. Responsible right is right to accept our responsibility in our society and perform it well. The right of a bus or other transport owners is to maintain the comfort of the passengers when they pay for the fare tickets. The transport owners have no right to pack the passengers illegally on the seats. The right of real estate owners is to give comfort to the tenants when they pay for it. The real estate owners will not deny facilities to the tenants. The tenants will use the facilities wisely.

## Privileges

Privileges are the rights we enjoy in our society because of the position we hold in the society. A worker's privilege is his salary and other enjoyments accorded to him because of his work. The denial of privileges reduces the incentive to work. This is one of the reasons we have poor production in Nigeria. When a worker's privileges are given to him or her, the worker has no excuse in giving his or her services. But if a worker's privileges are denied to him or her, the worker will spend more time in fighting for the privileges and less time at work. The improper administration of promotion reduces the incentives of good workers. But proper administration of promotions induces people to work hard, and even corrects the bad workers. The inadequate distribution of goods and services results in indisciplined lines. The order or system is destroyed when there is any proof of favouritism. Nobody likes to be in a line and someone behind him is served and he is not. War against lack of discipline will be war of self-examination. When an individual is disciplined, it means that the society is disciplined.

A person has the privileged right to tools of performance when he or she is employed in an office. The tools must be for office use and not for selfish ends. When a person is suspected in any way, the person should not be employed. But when a person is finally employed, the person should not be suspected. Tools to be used in office performance are one of the drawbacks in employee performances in Nigeria. Some teachers do not have textbooks, some civil servants do not have tools to perform, and in most hospitals there are no drugs. All these are the privileged rights of the employee. They must be equipped with tools so as to be able to perform. Before we blame somebody for wrongdoing we will try to find out why somebody does what he or she does. But a person who persistently performs good services in the midst of bad odds is a mature responsible citizen. This person is a nationalist. A person who abuses the privileged rights is a traitor to the nation. We are ambassadors of good will where-ever we are.

## Political Morality

The practicing politicians make politics an unaccepted philosophy by many good people. There is a general concensus of people that politics is a dirty game. Political morality tries to point out some facts about politics which some people ignore. Politics is a struggle for power. Power by itself is not bad. What is bad is the abuse of power. When power is employed in a right way there will be ethics in politics. The right political power is the power to protect the people. This means all the people and not some of the people. An ethical politician will use his power to protect all people, including those who are against him. So a politician will know that he is responsible to all the people in his society, that is, those people who voted for him or voted against him. But once he is voted into power, all these people become his people. He will protect their interests and they in turn will support him. By the same reasoning the right power is to protect the public property. Protecting public property does not mean using the property for selfish ends. The public property will be protected for public use.

A moral politician pursues the interest of his nation. The national interest must be the protection of his nation's territorial integrity, maintaining the civil liberty and civil rights of the people, and maintaining equality under the law in his country.

# Part IV

# Religious Development

# Chapter 13
# Religion and Philosophy

## Religion and Nigerian Nationalism

### Religion

The family that prays together stays together. The nation that serves one philosophy together stays together.

We serve God through Christ or we serve God through the Prophet Mohammad. In like manner we serve Nigeria through the state. No one can serve his or her state and despise Nigeria and no one can serve Nigeria and neglect his or her state. While serving our states we serve Nigeria. By the same token while serving our local governments we serve our state and we serve Nigeria. This is the philosophical reasoning leading to unity and continuity of services to one's nation. If all the states in Nigeria are developed except one, Nigeria is still an undeveloped country. Therefore let us work together for the unity and development of Nigeria. Stable persons make stable families, and stable families make a stable society and a stable nation. The stable society is developed from the cultural pattern of the society. But culture is built on religion. Before a stable society is discussed, religion must come into the discussion. The ancient leaders of the primitive age were the religious leaders. In order to deal with the religious development, we have to look into the belief that holds people together. The belief that holds people together can be found in the way the people are corrected if there is wrong doing, the way they act in response to age, the way they worship, and the link of the society. All these could help to determine the kind of stability in any society.

Rome was the leader of the world. Britain challenged Roman leadership and broke off from the Roman religious administration. The early Christians were persecuted because of their religious beliefs. We observed in history more religious wars and persecutions than we observed economic wars. Economic wars are short-lived wars. Once people find enough to eat, the economic war ends. But religious war never stopped. It went on after the generations involved were gone. Religion controls mankind. When you read this, pause and think how you feel about your religion. Ask yourself what influence your religion has on you: your communication with people, your friendly relationships, your marriage and your ideas about the world and the people around you. The most stable nation today is the nation that gives a pragmatic treatment to religion. The United States of America believes in the separation of church and state. That is, religion has nothing to do with state affairs. For example in the state of Maryland a woman took the public school system to court because her child was asked to pray. The judge, presumably a Christian, deemed her right in the case. In Latin American countries the instability is partly due to religious misunderstandings. One of the most stable nations in the world: Great Britain is in trouble at this time of her social advancement because of religious misgivings. In Nigeria one sect of the Moslem religion set out to slaughter other sects because of a minute religious misunderstanding.

However civilized we are, religion still plays an important role on our life. The challenge to world civilization is religion. To my opinion the best religion is one's affair with one's God which is made perfect or expressed by one's attitude to one's fellow beings.

Religion will help to bind the minds of a nation to beliefs that will help in developing the country. Nationalism is the religion that does that job. Nationalism places the national leaders at the top of the nation as the religious leaders of ancient times were put at the top of the affairs of their society.

## Nigerian Nationalism

Nationalism is the religion of any nation. The religion of nationalism is observed according to the culture of the nation. This makes the nationalism of any nation a religion peculiar to that nation. But all nationalism has something in common. All aim at the unity of the nation and respect to the laws of the nation. Nigerian nationalism will work on the unity of Nigeria; tribalism and other religious differences will give way to Nigerian nationalism. Nigerian nationalism although it will be highly observed by the people, will not interfere with religious practices where the practices do not infringe on the national interest of Nigeria. The worship of Nigerian nationalism is that all Nigerians must be honest to Nigeria. Nigerians will seek for the unity and peace of Nigeria, and defend the interest of Nigeria. Nigeria nationalism is the practical approach to the reality of all the religions. Nigerian nationalism will have a liberal approach to religious instruction. The religious instruction should be open to all the students. Christians can take Koran courses, and Moslems can take Christian religious courses. This will bring more understanding to the students about each others' beliefs. The moral instruction lessons will occur on a national basis. Stories and lessons that promote peace and unity will be delivered during the moral instruction lessons. Moral instruction is the course that will inculcate nationalism into the students. Students will behave like the students of one country and not like the students of different countries. My religious course at Oberlin College under Professor Long broadened my religious understanding because the world's religions were taught and not a particular religion. This brought a better relationship with other religious groups. Nationalism as a religion does not mean that other religions will be overlooked. Nationalism helps to observe other religions as they should be. Nationalism will bring more understanding to other religions, and this will foster peace and unity in the country.

Nationalism is a difficult philosophy to practice in developing nations. The reason is that nationalism has dual functions to perform before it is fully understood in a nation. One is the state's function and another is the people's function. Any state that wants the loyalty of the nationals must first show interest in the people. The state must realize that it is her responsibility to take care of the people in her territorial area. Territorial integrity means the ability of a nation to defend her territory, that is, its boundary area and the people and properties. The condition of the people in a country is the responsibility of the leaders of the country. When the people realize that the state is interested in their affairs, they will be loyal to the state.

## Function of the People

When we talk about Nigeria, we mean the area and the people. The people are more important than the area. When the people are honest, it means that Nigeria is an honest country. The people in Nigeria will make Nigeria what they want Nigeria to be. The people will build Nigeria by obeying the policies of the country. The people will realize that the state is interested in them. That is why she makes policies to protect, develop, and build Nigeria for them. This understanding brings loyalty to the country. Loyalty means that they obey and serve the country. Obedience and service means that people do the right thing and help others to do the right thing. Any person who overlooks a wrong doer is not serving his or her country. Nationalism will be practiced as a religion. When we do the right things, we correct the wrong things or report the wrongs to the appropriate area. When we mind our own business and never care what a wicked person does, we are not being good nationalists. Nigerian nationalism will be an honest effort to serve the country by committing ourselves to the national interest and seeing that others likewise commit themselves to the national interest.

# Chapter 14
# Philosophy of Morality

Religion and philosophy are the unforseen areas of development. They build faith and confidence in oneself and transfer the faith and confidence to others. The faith and confidence of others results in nationalism. Any person who is not nationalistic cannot trust others and cannot trust himself.

The national religious development is manifested in politics and economics. Religion takes place in the mind and helps in political and economic behaviours of the people. This is why dogmatic religion is very dangerous. Dogmatism pursues unrealistic philosophy. The kind of religion favourable for political development is the religion that pursues the liberal relationships between people.

## Liberalism

Liberalism is a philosophy formulated by protesting Christians which emphasized intellectual liberty and the spiritual and ethical content of Christianity. Liberalism does not mean taking sides with evil or protecting the wickedness of people. Liberalism may ally with goodness in a person in order to correct the person's evil. Any person has both good and bad qualities. No person is completely bad or completely good. The work of liberalism is to ally with the good quality in a human being and correct the bad quality. The good quality is the ethical content of a person. This part of the human being will be highly exploited in order to have a cordial understanding with people. This is what liberalism does. It does not condone evil, it joins with goodness to fight the evil. It does not condemn the sins of the people but it tries to expose the people to righteousness. This exposure to righteousness helps them to abhor sin. This is seen in Christ's life in the world. He said, "Neither do I condemn you but go home and sin no more." Christ moved freely with the sinners, but their sins never influenced his life. Instead his life influenced the people to good works and repentance. Liberalism can change a thief by employing the strength used in stealing to perform productive activities generally accepted by the people. This is what liberalism does to politics and economics. Liberalism directs the economic wealth and political power to serve the nation. It gives to God that which is God's and to Caesar that which is Caesar's.

# Chapter 15
# Africanism

The OAU (Organization for African Unity) has been functioning without its own philosophy. There are different philosophies from the African heads of states. Capitalist oriented philosophies are struggling with socialist oriented philosophies. Such a situation cannot afford stable unity. There are tendencies of blackmailing a country due to its inclination to East or West. This should be put under control by adopting a separate brand name of philosophy which will spell out African interests unaffliated to either East or West. But such interests will be both unbiased and uncommitted. It will not be bent to the East because the East has not much in common with Africa. It will not lean to the West because the West has a dominating notion about Africa. East or West looks upon Africa as prey that will either go to the East or go to the West. African philosophy will dispel all these philosophies and create one that will unite African countries and still maintain friendly relationship with the East or the West.

Africa is a black continent, that is, Africa has a great majority of black people, but Africa does not oust the white minority. African philosophy will accommodate and mingle with the white minority. The lack of united philosophy by the OAU places the majority under the control of minority. The minority of whites on the continent controls the black majority. The white nations outside the continent control the black nations within the continent. Africa should be for Africans and Africanism should be Africa's philosophy. Africanism loves all and hates no one. Africanism will make its laws and enforce them. Africa has resources for its law enforcement. It has nothing to lose but much to gain when it becomes united. The unity of Africa will contribute to the peace of the world. The East and West will rest easy because they'll know that no amount of diplomacy or money will woo Africa to East or to West.

Africanism will not be a neutral philosophy because it must involve Africa in what concerns African interests. The involvement of Africanism is that of understanding and not misunderstanding, understanding because it has a liberal attitude towards other countries and continents. It explains itself as a protector of African interests to any degree acceptable by African nations. The OAU will include all the countries in Africa and protect all the peoples in Africa. The exclusion of the white-ruled countries from the OAU makes the OAU an imperfect organization to deal with the African interests. The inclusion of the white-ruled countries will bring more understanding and mutual coexistence of all people on the continent. The inclusion of the white-ruled countries in the OAU will help in developing a kind of understanding that will bring peace with the neighboring black-ruled countries. The whites will be made to understand that the unity is not meant to oust anybody but to join hands in developing the countries. The whites and the blacks will bring their knowledge and spread it all over the countries to develop all the areas. The blacks will understand that the unity is not one of domination. No race will lord it over other races. The unity is not one of dirty politics. Political morality will be studied and practiced. When this is applied, a qualified person not a race will rule the countries. The blacks will understand that their majority is not a strength to destroy the countries, but one to building the countries. OAU will develop the policy of checks and balances for all the countries in their unity.

When these countries are stable, there will be no question about future development. American strength and philosophy will be emulated by any nation that has many different peoples. Cordiality that exists in America cannot be if there is no understanding between the peoples of America. There was a time when suggestion of creating a separate black state in the United States of America was rumoured, but such ideas were dismissed in favour of mixed states. There is no doubt that a separate black state or such similar ideas will be a creator of instability in any place it exists. Such separate colour states will contribute to the inroad of external enemies. OAU will seek for a policy or policies that will bring all the countries of Africa under the protection of the OAU. It will be an organization of African states—to include black and white states.

# Chapter 16
# The Disposal of Refuse

While discussing production and consumption in aid to economic development, the refuse has its contribution to development. Refuse is an eyesore when it is exposed to the public and it makes a mess when it is hidden. For a realistic dealing in development, refuse disposal will be treated to ensure a complete treatment in development. Lack of this keeps a place undeveloped. In developing countries it is not uncommon to see feces in some corners of public places like the hospital. The people urinate wherever because there is no place for it. All this adds to the undeveloped nature of the developing countries.

Since strong emphasis is put on production and consumption, I want to point out that equal emphasis should be put on the disposal of production wastes to complete the social development. Waste products are the most difficult problems in an industrialized countries. The pollution of air and water are the outcome of the waste products. When a dynamic social development tries to introduce stable development, the stability will be challenged by accumulated wastes. The dynamic social development therefore tries to develop an idea that there is no waste. Any waste is an input to another production. This completes a stable development. What we think to be a waste can be an input to another product. For example, chicken droppings can be used to produce manure for crops in cultivation. Human feces can be treated in that way too. Old pans and old steel and iron can be reused after processing them. Old papers and books can be burned and ashes used. Any material we think is useless can be turned to a useful purpose by a developed mind. When the mind is developed, all the resources can be developed by the developed mind whether raw materials or waste materials. The system will be a cycle.

# Chapter 17
# Developed Countries

Development is a word used by societies all over the world. In this book efforts have been made to discuss the developing countries and not the developed societies. The beginning of development is the change of mind from the old society and readiness to work towards a new society. Such growing awareness must possess the knowledge essential to exploit the cultures of the society and develop them with the available resources.

When we come to the developed society, questions come to mind. Is it a full or partial development? Is any society fully developed? Development, like civilization, can never be full. We speak of degrees of development. But there is a degree or condition which will be met and the society will be regarded as a developed society. This condition has its interpretation in the welfare state and morality, the condition in which the government allocates primary amenities to reach all the areas of the society whether poor or rich. These amenities are enjoyed by all, but they are not financed by all. The primary amenities are: good roads, good water supply, electricity, good communications and health programs. The people will build acceptable houses for themselves. The moral condition of developed society is such that an individual will feel secure and feel at home wherever the individual is within his or her country. The employment is on merits, qualifications of knowledge and skill, and knowhow; and not on nepotism, tribalism, and sectionalism. The individuals in offices feel the obligation of service to any person and not the glory of the post or position occupied. The policy is for all and not for a privileged few.

In developing countries the individuals try to develop themselves by supplying good houses, electricity and sink wells. After all these, they still remain an undeveloped society because the primary amenities do not reach all the members of the society. Some build mansions with electricity and water but no good roads. So when the society has good roads, a good water supply, electricity, good communication, and a good health system, the society has attained an acceptable degree of development to be called a developed society. Also there will be a system of continuity of maintainence to assure that the development will not break down. There will be also a system of changes in the political offices to avoid one person or set of people dominating them.

The rest of the amenities are secondary ones which will be added as time goes on. They will not disturb the developed condition when the primary ones are in operation.

But development will never be full. We have beggars even in the streets of developed nations. Robbers roam the cities causing discomfort and fear in the people. Unemployment exists, making for uncertainty. These are examples of the areas that are challenging to experts in development.

# Chapter 18
# Conclusion

Development is a change from one condition to another. It begins with the development of mind and goes to production, consumption, and distribution of resources. This means destabilization of society. In a given social condition of equilibrium, development means disturbing the equilibrium and creating a better equilibrium. These conditions can be achieved in different ways depending upon the kind of philosophy applied in the change. The foundation philosophy is very important. The philosophy of selfishness accumulates wealth in a way that instability develops in the society. But the inclusion of the philosophy of liberalism and checks and balances results in smooth changes. The social changes can be viewed in this way: First that a kind of equality exists levelling the society to the same standard of living. The second is destabilization that accumulates heaps at one end and creates troughs at the other end. The third is how to destabilize the heaps and create an acceptable social level. This is the cycle of accumulation and deaccumulation. A society with checked social systems will make policies that help in the reallocation of the resources. This is the function of fiscal policy. Society with the unchecked social system lives to see bloody revolution. There is nothing that will solve the problems of unchecked accumulation but bloody revolution. The human being is an envious animal and there is a stage where his enviousness can explode in a dangerous temper tantrum.

Dynamic social development presents smooth changes

to a stable development. Dynamism in development is how the resources will be employed to solve the problems facing development. This begins with a change of mind. This is the development of mind which will build a kind of acceptable development by the society. The discussions and analyses make the writer conclude that the philosophy that will give the kind of dynamic development he is talking about is a liberal philosophy. Since socialism refers to the society it is not a beginner of development. It cannot help the developing countries. Socialism is a stage to be attained in development and not a beginner. Capitalism pertains to individuals and it is the individual who begins, so capitalism is a beginner. So liberal capitalism will help in peaceful stable development. Joseph Schumpeter maintained that if morality can be included in capitalism it will be the best philosophy to give an acceptable development.

The dynamic social development has been discussed vis à vis political morality and social morality and the conclusion is that the roots of development are peace, unity, and honesty. If these are not put into practice, there will be a cycle of unsolved problems in development. Morality can be introduced through impartiality of policy administration. Policies are made for all, not for a special group of people.

The developing countries will learn from the mistakes of the developed countries. However vicious a society is, early checks will correct it. The reason why there were heaps of accumulation in one end and troughs at the other end in developed nations was due to allocation of resources. The bourgeoisie possessed all land and productive tools, while the proletarian possessed only labour. So the products went to the person who financed most of the production. The dynamic social development maintains that a farmer will possess his land, tools, and crops or livestock. The degree of the possession does not matter. This means that a farmer will receive his product according to the degree of his investment.

**Table of Stages of Dynamic Social Process and Stability**

| Stages | Internal, Invisible | External, Visible |
|---|---|---|
| 1. Developing process | In the mind, the root of development: Peace, Honesty, Unity | Physically: roads, water, electricity, communications and health. |
| 2. Maintenance process | Checks and balances to social phenomena | Maintenance of the physical projects |
| 3. Growth process | Welfare scheme: the beggars and underprivileged. | Mechanization, inventions, research and development |

The selling of labour will be minimized to a degree that a poor farmer, whether he sells his labour or not, is detached morally from the big farmer who buys his labour. The farmer has the pride of producing his own products. The developing countries will not encourage gigantic farming from the outset because it will disturb agricultural development. These giant farmers cannot feed the nation when the little farmers are pushed out due to cutthroat competition. The little farmers will be encouraged to stay on the farm through a policy of assistance, loans, and/or grants. The dynamic social development encourages cottage industries. The private control of giant manufacturing industries will not occur when the government owns more than sixty percent of industry's shares. This will assure the labour class be respected as human beings instead of being dehumanized by the owners of big industries. Labour will not be treated as articles of production competing with capital.

With good fiscal policy in addition to the above points, morality will be introduced into capitalism and it will be checked. Large accumulation will be moderated. Labour will be a part of the society and not attached to the wealthy people. Labour cannot be converted into capital. Labour becomes free. The bourgeois power will be reduced, since the government has the largest economic power. The bourgeoisie will look upon the labouring class as fellow members of the society, and not as tools of production.